Chapter 1

The night was reasonably cool, and there was an African American couple, a man and a very pregnant woman sitting on a tatty red couch.

***

The man, Amos, worked in construction and the woman, Deirdre, worked at a diner waiting tables. The child yet to be born wasn't an excitement; they were dreading the impact it would have – how it would be disrupting their lives and put a strain on their finances.

The couple wasn't particularly well off, which was one of the nicest ways of saying that they were poor. They could almost always afford their necessities, which included enough for Amos to have one bottle of beer a night. The nightly beer was a tradition his wife allowed, and it was the thing that he wanted to give up the least – it helped him deal with his days at work. It was a stroke of luck that Amos had finally gotten the promotion he'd been working towards, and thankfully it came with a small pay rise. Hopefully, it would be enough because their two-person household was about to become a household of three.

Deirdre had been working right up until a week before the baby's due date. A due date that had passed over two weeks before. The couple were angry that it was late, and they were already holding it against their unborn child; it was difficult for a couple who prided themselves on their punctuality that their child was late.

Their neighborhood wasn't affluent. It was a bad neighborhood located about an hour and a half from the city center. The neighborhood was full of rough edges, the odd gunshots in the night, loose teeth in the gutters, drying blood on paths, and the indigo bruises on the skin that faded to the yellow of flowering weeds in sidewalk cracks.

This wasn't out of the ordinary; it was normal – well, it was their normal.

***

They could hear the rhythm of cars backfiring and the tires burning as the late-night races revved to life. Amos sipped his beer; their little television crackled with life. Then Deirdre grunted and shifted slightly where she sat.

"We need to go," she said in a firm voice. Amos looked at her blankly before taking a sip of his beer; his face lit up by the lights of the television.

"Go where? There is nothing going on," he turned back to the screen.

"My water broke," she stated bluntly.

"I'll go to the kitchen and get you another glass," he said, misunderstanding and mishearing her completely.

"No! you moron. My water broke. This baby is coming," she groaned.

"Ah.." he swallowed, "right. Hospital then."

"Yes, hospital," she grunted deeply as she tried to pull herself up from the couch. She glared at him when all he did was watch her.

"Right. I'll help," his words came out stuttered, and he stood up fast. His beer bottle still held in the tight grip of his hand, Amos gulped down the dregs and then helped his wife to their car. Their car was old; the paint which had once been the same blue as the label for Spam, was now sun-faded and just beginning to blister and crack; thankfully, the car ran well.

**

The Hospital, a multipurpose building that served as a clinic, GP, and Hospital all in one. The building itself is an uninspiring brown block; the windows and doors provided grey accents. There were thin bars over all the glass on the ground floor, acting as protection from stone projectiles, which had been frequently thrown through them. After the bars were added, people had just aimed their stones for the glass on the higher levels. The security was patchy; the cameras weren't always working. The Hospital consisted of four levels, including the ground floor, and was situated on a straight stretch of road that was used almost nightly as part of the drag races.

*

Amos parked the car and silently worried that the drag races would damage his vehicle. Awkwardly he helped his wife out of the car, but when he tried helping her to the Hospital, she slapped his hands away.
"Don't forget to grab the bag," she growled; one had resting tense against her stomach.

"Sorry," he muttered as he grabbed the bulging duffle bag. He closed the door and locked the car before tripping after his wife, who was hobbling remarkably fast towards the Hospital's entrance.

****

The birth itself was routine and natural. Deirdre's knuckles were white as she squeezed Amos's hand, her breathing ragged and pained. Amos winced in pain but kept his mouth shut – Deirdre had already snarled at him multiple times, once was to tell him that she 'was giving birth and therefore he could keep his man pain to himself.' When the child was finally born and breathing in the air around them, he felt himself relax; that was until the baby started crying out loudly

**

"Do you have a name for her?" the nurse asked with her black pen poised over a clipboard.

"What?" Amos and Deirdre said at the same time.
"Do you have a name for your baby girl?" the nurse repeated.
"Wasn't expecting a girl child," Amos stated while looking at the wrinkly soft-looking thing in his wife's arm. His wife, Deirdre, was looking at the bundle in her arms as if she wasn't quite sure what to make of it.
"…Right. I'll give the two of you some time together to think of a name for that joyful little girl," the nurse put her pen into one of her pockets and held the clipboard to her crisp uniform as she left the room and closed the door behind her.

Apart from the quiet snuffling of the baby, silence settles over the room.

"Samantha," Amos blurted out of the blue, breaking the quiet.
"What?" Deirdre replied.
"As a name for that thing," he said, pointing at the baby.

"Our daughter, you mean?" she looked at him with an expression that he couldn't quite name.

"Yes, yes. So? What do you think of Samantha as a name?"

"Wasn't that the name on the tag of the nurse who just left?" she asked him with one eyebrow raised.
"I couldn't think of anything else," he defended.

"Really?" she snorted and hummed to herself.
"I hadn't considered that it would be girl," he said.

"There was a fifty/fifty chance of our baby being a girl," Deirdre said with a roll of her eyes, "you have no other names to suggest?"
"Ummm," Amos uttered, before muttering loudly, "And anyway, since when do you care? We didn't even want a kid. What are we going to do now that we have one?"
"Live with her," she sighed, "What do you think of Emma, for a name?"

"Not really a name that would fit in our neighborhood," he said half-heartedly.

"...Sarah?" she suggested.
"Sounds like the name for someone with more than we have; I feel like it's the name of someone with pearls, expensive clothes, and racist comments."

Deirdre scoffed, "that is ridiculous. Sarah might not be the right name, but there are some perfectly nice Sarah's in our neighborhood."

"We could name her Olive," he recommended.
"We aren't naming her after one of your favorite pizza toppings," she glared at him with sharp but tired eyes.

"It was just a suggestion."
"Lilly or possibly Tilly?" she questioned; her brow furrowed.
"No, too flowery," he wrinkled his nose as if someone had shoved a bunch of flowers under his nose, and he was revolted by the smell, "How about Tamara? it's not a bad name."

"Doesn't feel quite right," she responded.

"Doesn't feel right. Nothing feels right anymore. Besides, it's a name; she will grow into it. What does it matter what her name is anyway?"

"What's in a name?" she murmured, gently running her finger across the baby's crown of fine and downy hair.
"Is that one of your uppity book quotes?" he mumbled grumpily.
She hummed, ignoring him.
Amos sighed and then groaned in frustration, "We could just name her Kila," he suggested with a shrug.
"No. I don't think so," she said strongly. She started humming again, and for a while, silence fell between them. Then she spoke clearly,

"Iesha, I think," she said, eyes finally looking interested in the baby that laid in her arms.

****

In the very beginning, Iesha, the little baby with dark skin, was loved. The two new parents were surprised to find themselves growing fond of their new daughter. She was the only change in their lives, and they lived in their little house, still affording most of their necessities. Sometimes Amos had to go without his nightly beer, which he was not happy about. But it was their new normal. That is, until everything changed. Situations and circumstance started shifting, things got darker, and so dawned a new normal.

**

 The first change that happened involved Amos's mother, Maude, moving into their only spare room when Iesha was four and a half.
Maude hadn't been able to pay the utilities and had in the end lost the house she had lived in since she had gotten married, it held all the memories of her late husband, and it was where they had raised their five children – including Amos. Maude was a stern, small-statured woman who was hard to please and whose words were almost always cutting. She cursed and ranted at the small family any chance that she had. According to her, Amos could have done better than Deirdre, the waitress, a waitress who hadn't been raised in a proper household. Maude didn't have kind words for anyone. Her son was hopeless; he was a disappointment – the constant scorn she aimed at her son made his hands shake and deeply rely on his bottle of nightly beer. Amos's wife Deirdre was so frequently battered by Maude's harsh words that she stopped defending herself as strongly and started curling into herself. Both leaving their young daughter to fend for herself against her grandmother's words and attitude.

**

The second biggest change happened after Iesha had just turned six, and Maude had been living with them and cursing them out for well over a year.
It was a warm evening, and there was the sound of beetles on the breeze.

The surprisingly tranquil night, if you ignored Maude's acidic muttering about loud pests, was broken by a loud, rapid knocking on the front door.

"Answer it, girl," Maude demanded, waving her hand at Deirdre. Deirdre scowled at both Maude and her husband - who just sat there with his beer in his hand, but she stood up and walked to the front door. She slid the lock and had barely pulled open the door when it was pushed completely open by a neatly manicured hand.

"You don't mind, do you?" a voice said, and Deirdre found herself looking at her sister, Carley. Carley was dressed impeccably, and she swept in without Care; her husband Timothy trailed in after her, stumbling with the weight of their bags and with a frown on his face. He opened his mouth to speak, but no sound was heard because Carley had started throwing out orders.

"Where is our room, Deiry?" her mouth was tightening with disgust as she examined the small house she'd just entered.
"We do, in fact, mind Carley. Amos's mother is already living in what used to be our only spare room," Deirdre was furious at her older sister, "What do you need a room for anyway? You have a house. Multiple houses if I remember your bragging correctly. You and your husband live in the city where the lights are bright, and money flies from your hands."

Carley pouted, "Our accounts are temporarily closed, there was some stupid embezzlement thing at work, and absolutely everyone is under investigation," she said dramatically. She looked around her. "Well, this will have to change," she said, "that thing you are using as a lounge…"

"You mean the couch we are using as a lounge," Deirdre interrupted, deadpan. Carley waved her had "whatever, it has to go, and you clearly need to hire a new cleaner. It's filthy in here."

"Carley, stop it," Timothy said in a clear voice.

"What's for dinner," she ignored him. "Show us our room, sis," she finished by widening her eyes and pouting.

"Stop the act Carley, that has never worked on me, and I don't think it works on your husband either" Deirdre was already tired of her big sister's presence, "The lounge you are complaining about is younger than Iesha."

"Who?" Carley asked with a blank expression. Timothy pinched the bridge of his nose "Our niece," he said, and at the same time, Deirdre answered, "My daughter."

She waved a hand at her daughter, who had walked herself over to where Timothy was standing and was now holding onto the fabric of his pants and looking up at the man with her head tipped to the side curiously. Timothy was looking down at Iesha with a mix of surprise, excitement, and trepidation.
Deirdre wondered at his expression for a moment but then ignored it to deal with her sister.

"We don't hire a cleaner, Carley. I clean and Maude, my mother in law, cleans when she isn't satisfied with the job I've done. She's even taught Iesha to clean. We don't have large bank accounts here; we don't have the money to support your extravagant tastes or lifestyle."
"Where does that brat live then?" Carley said with a disgruntled sneer.
"My daughter lives here in this house; she has her own room," Dierdre sighed.

"Timothy and I will take her room then.."
"No, we won't," he interrupted her, frustration lacing his features.
"Shush, darling," she mocked before turning back to the conversation she was having with her sister. "Your brat, Issa, was it…"

"Iesha," her husband muttered. The little girl at his leg giggled and smiled at him. He returned the smile tiredly.

"Whatever. The brat can sleep out here on that lounge thing," then Carley smile brightly, and Timothy groaned silently, "Or even better," she said, "I'm sure the brat can sleep outside."

"Carley!!" both Timothy and Deirdre said at the same time. Timothy's tone of voice was scolding, while Deirdre sounded tired and almost reluctant.

Ignoring them, Carley said, "We're family, little sister; you can't say no."

Now Deirdre was angry, "Why not? You have always said no to me. In the past, when I asked for a money loan or for help, you said NO—every single time. Now here you are, with your husband, expecting me to fold to your every whim, expecting us to house you. Not only that, but it sounds like you want us to support you monetarily as well."

"Oh, good you understood, I did wonder. Of course, I'm expecting that our accounts are closed at the moment."

"Get jobs," Deirdre demanded.

"We had jobs," Carley's voice came out in a whine. The two sisters fell silent. Maude was watching them like her favorite soap opera, and Amos looked angry that he couldn't hear the television.

Timothy spoke up, his voice strong and clear in the room.
"I don't expect to stay here for free. I have every intention of finding a job; my wife and I can camp in your backyard," he paused and looked sternly at his wife before focusing clear blue eyes on Deirdre, "It would appear that my wife has been telling lies about you and your family, not only that but keeping quiet about you needing help or a loan. I wasn't aware you asked for either on any occasion and if I had known, I would have assisted you. You are my sister-in-law; that makes you family, and to me, family is the most important thing in our lives".

Iesha's world had just been drastically altered. Unbeknownst to her, it would get darker, and the only Good would be the presence of Uncle Timothy in her life.

CHAPTER 2

Iesha clearly remembered the day that her Aunt Carley and Uncle Timothy moved into the house and took over her room, relegating her to the couch, the back porch, or a spare piece of floor. She remembered how her mum and dad became mother and father, then Amos and Deirdre, and how they balked at Carley's presence. Her aunt was a spiteful woman who valued appearance; she did not like Iesha calling her Aunt, Auntie, or anything familiar – she told Iesha to call her Carley or ma'am. Carley's husband, Timothy, seemed to be her polar opposite; he was an intelligent man with blue eyes, patience, and kindness. His skin wasn't as dark as Iesha's; it reminded her of chocolate milk rather than chocolate cake. His smile had been bright and overjoyed when she had called him Uncle Tim. Carley had scowled and tried to shut that familiarity down; "his name is Timothy, you little weed."

Her Uncle had growled right back at her, "Why don't you stop being ridiculous, Care. If you'll deign to remember, I wanted kids, but I literally can't have them. I certainly remember the look in your eyes when those tests came back that said I would be able to father a child; your relief hurt our relationship. But we worked past it; you brushed it off as it meant life was going your way, and you didn't need to compromise, and I grieved, and then I signed up to the big brother program."

"Timothy.." Carley started to say.

"No, Carley," he stated strongly before looking at Iesha, whose head had been bouncing between the two arguing adults, "I'd be honored to be called Uncle Tim, but whatever you feel comfortable with, Iesha."

******

Iesha's young life, her would-be happy childhood was marred by her neighborhood and the adults in her life. The neighborhood they lived in wasn't what you would call a good one; most of the people were on the poorer side, and violence littered the streets. She could walk down the street and violence was on the street corners, it was at diner tables, in couple walking, you could even see it through people's windows. There was dried blood-splattered and badly cleaned up; sometimes, there was the odd tooth on the path. None of this was out of the ordinary in Iesha's world – it was normal.

Violence and abuse seeped into the house; it had begun with Maude, then Carley, and then her father Amos and her mother, Deirdre. Iesha and Timothy bonded and drew closer, standing together against the others– for what little Good that did.

The first four and a half years of her life, her early childhood, was full of color and being cared for – but had slowly been leached of color, and there was a bleakness that settled over the lives of both Iesha and her Uncle Tim.

***

Carley put off finding a job as long as she could, dithering and faffing about whenever it was brought up amongst the adults of the house. Timothy, on the other, had found a job at a primary school and volunteered at the community and youth center.

When Iesha started going to school, not long after turning six or the arrival of her aunt and uncle, it wasn't either of her parents who dropped her off or picked her up.

It was her Uncle. When he went to work, she went with him, and when school was over, she would wait until he picked her up. Some people didn't realize that her parents were alive or in her life at all because they never saw them.

Her Uncle Tim quickly became the only person and adult that she trusted.

****

Maude continued with her harsh diatribes, now including Carley and Timothy into them. Her bitterness and rants culminated with the odd hard slap when she felt the message hadn't sunk in. Amos might be her father, but it was safer for Iesha to call him by his name when they interacted; otherwise, he would flinch and glare at her angrily. He was still working construction, but now he was a functioning alcoholic, drinking far more than was wise. He and Carley spent more time together on the lounge or on the back porch bonding over alcohol.

*

Her mother, Deirdre, became more closed off as her husband drew closer to her big sister, and the two drifted apart as he sank into alcoholism. She worked long hours, spent less time in the house she had once called home, neglecting and forgetting the daughter she had briefly loved. Deirdre tended to keep quiet around the child she had birthed; it was partly guilt and partly that she was becoming indifferent.

When Iesha was six and had just started school, one Saturday, Deirdre had gotten so angry at everything that she had verbally lashed out at the little six-year-old girl, "I blame you. But I shouldn't blame you for all of this," she waved her hand around "You don't control my sister or your grandmother or your father. Hell." She muttered before continuing loudly, "If you didn't exist, they'd probably still be here in this house. Before you were born, I wished you hadn't existed; when you were first born, I loved you absolutely, now I mostly wish you didn't exist. Why do you need to exist?"

Timothy intervened when Dierdre's harsh words tapered off, "Deirdre, you can't really mean that." He didn't care if it sounded like he was begging her, "Deirdre Iesha is a child and a very bright child at that."

"Yeah, right," she said sardonically.

"Shut up, Timothy," Carley shouted from her seat in front of the television, never turning her head in their direction.

Timothy stepped up next to Iesha and curled an arm around her shoulder before picking her up and hugging her. She wrapped her too thin arms around his neck and buried her head into his shoulder; he felt his t-shirt dampen with tears.

*

The house was toxic – they all lived there, and barring Timothy and Iesha, the adults were like angry ghosts haunting the space and barely living. It was a relatively unhappy house to exist in.

****

Timothy had been halfway through high school when he decided he wanted to be a teacher, and he had worked hard towards his goal. His parents hadn't been happy and had tried to get him to drop out of his degree. Eventually, they came to a compromise and an understanding. He could finish his teaching degree if he also got a business degree.

He had begun doing a single degree, but halfway through his first year, he had turned it into a double degree. His parents wanted him to never be without and wanted him to follow in their footsteps by entering the corporate world. His mother had a health scare during his last year of study, and it had propelled and cemented the decision to go into the world of business to please his parents.

He had been good at his job and had worked hard to rise up in the corporate hierarchy; he was successful but not exactly happy. Then he had met Carley near the beginning of their times in the company; she had been a secretary less obsessed with money and status. Carley had also worked her way up in the business world, and she had become more interested in their status and how much money they had.

*

Living without access to his money and not living to the expensive means he had been used to had been brilliant for Timothy. It gave him freedom from a job he didn't like and a closer look at the person his wife actually was compared to who she pretended to be around him.

He'd been given a new lease on life and had embraced any changes and adapted to them as they came into his life.

*

After moving in with – Dierdre, Amos, Iesha, and Maude - he had gotten a job as a teacher. He was working the job he had wanted to work since he was a teenager. He wanted to help kids learn, grow, and prosper. The job he'd gotten had been at a public school that seemed to go through teachers like someone with a cold goes through tissues. He'd been told that the students were pointless and not worth the effort. Timothy had been quietly furious; he hated the idea of students being ignored and treated like they were stupid. It was a teacher's job to inspire.

After he met the other teachers on his first day, he became determined to make a difference within the school, even if that meant taking over.

He found that the teachers were, for the most part, dismissive, rude, and their treatment of the students was the same if not worse. Timothy was a reasonably positive person, and his excitement for his job and his determination was not popular with the other teachers, but he ignored it. He started to change things; it was small things in the beginning, but they gradually got bigger.

****

The household was tumultuous. Words were the main weapons that were fought with. But that didn't mean that physical violence wasn't used. Slaps were the most frequent and were deemed by the adults, bar her Uncle, to be the most effective. Iesha also received kicks to her ankles, and hard slaps and rough 'nudges' to deliver a message or to get her to move. As the attitudes of those living in the house grew harsher and darker, Iesha slowly stopped talking. She was mostly mute to all but her Uncle. He tried to interfere and stop their words and violence as things got worse, but the worsening relationship with his wife meant that the tides soon turned against him too.

The verbal and physical assault now included him, and he made sure he had evidence of the physical abuse by taking photos because if he ever goes around to filing for a divorce, the photos would help his case.

His wife believed that he was doing everything wrong; she whined and threw her tantrums – according to her, he should be pampering her and worshipping her every action and word, even without having access to their accounts.

**

The constant belittling that Iesha was subject to meant that she grew a thick shell.

'Worthless'

'What a Waste of space.'

'She'd be better off dead.'

*

'Why didn't you abort her.'
'Neither of us believed in that, remember.'
'It would have been better if you'd miscarried.'
Her Uncle did all he could to provide and give her positive reinforcement.

*

Her teachers and peers were no better with their words or actions. Bullying words were rained down upon her.
'Stupid girl.'

'Idiot'
'Dumb child.'

'Little bitch'
'Brat'
'What's the point of teaching you maths? It would be more useful to send you to the janitor for teaching. Cleaning is probably one of the only jobs you could get.'

During her first year of school, one teacher had said to her, *'I shouldn't have to teach people like you.'*

'What, female or black?' she had asked timidly.
'Ugh, both. Go away, you pest'.

****

Iesha was intelligent, not just that; she was clever. She noticed a lot about the world around her. Observing was her secret superpower and her weapon.

She flinched when she was hit – the faces of the abusers flickered with satisfaction and joy. Her pain was fun for them; if she didn't show them that it hurt, the hits got worse. But it was also a double-edged problem; sometimes they said, 'it's just a little slap, stop being so dramatic,' 'don't be a wimp, it doesn't hurt,' and 'what are you flinching for?'.

Other than words, her grandmother used a solid wooden spoon or a ruler as her weapon of choice. Maude thought that Iesha needs to understand proper etiquette and manners, as she saw it:

'Manners and etiquette are important, you unruly girl, especially for a woman.'

She would say, 'I will not have some uncouth hussy in my family.'

The ruler was used to rap her knuckles and hands, leaving red welts, and Iesha or her Uncle would sneak ice from the freezer for her hands.

The wooden spoon was whacked against her clothed backside; the older woman seemed to think these methods would get the message across.

Being backhanded across the face wasn't out of the ordinary for Iesha or for her Uncle. Carley felt it was a suitable way to deal with him, and it didn't help him when he witnessed anger between Iesha and one of the other adults and step between Iesha and the hand coming towards her.

Carley, her aunt, would try to force glasses of alcohol and cigarettes into Iesha's unwilling hands.

'You might as well learn at some point why not now,' Carley would say.

Iesha refused her every time by saying either"no" or "no thank you, ma'am."

It infuriated the woman, and she tended to backhand Iesha as punishment for refusing her. If her aunt became incandescent with rage, which generally happened after far more alcohol than was sensible, Carley would grab tightly onto Iesha's arm and press the glowing ember end of her cigarette against the skin. Thankfully, that was a practice that didn't last long because Tim caught her at it, and Iesha learned how to escape and avoid her when she was in that particular mood.

When Iesha decided that it was vital for her to learn and understand body language and how to recognize the many signs, she asked for her Uncle's help, and the two of them were conscientious in their study. It became almost instinctive and aided them in surviving their environment: the house, school, and the neighborhood.

There were so many different ways that the body could indicate emotions like anger. Sometimes an action would have more than one meaning, but if there were the pairing of multiple actions, it made it far easier to read a person.

Anger could be seen in:

The tightening of the jaw when a person grits their teeth.

Tense hard eyes.

Furrowed brows or angled eyebrows.

The clenching and unclenching of a person's fists.

The whiter the knuckles appeared, the tighter their fists were clenched.

To help further protect herself, her Uncle Tim ensured that she knew self-defense. He taught her in the little backyard when he knew that they wouldn't be bothered by the house's other occupants. He taught her how to lessen the impact of attacks and protect herself from both hits and hits being too damaging.

*

Iesha started her period comparatively early, she was nine, and on a basic level, she understood what was happening and what it meant for her body. She steeled herself, scared and worried, before venturing to find the women living in the house. She found her mother, grandmother, and aunt all sitting at the dining table; they had playing cards out, drinks of golden liquid, and an ashtray with stubbed out cigarettes. They were, to Iesha's surprise, being civil with each other. She stood and looked at them, twisting her hands together. They didn't notice her, engrossed in playing their game.

'Um M…' she tried to speak through her nerves. No reaction came.

Then her grandmother looked up

'What?'

The other women's head snapped around to look at her, irritation in all their eyes.

'Well, girl?' Deirdredemanded

'I'm bleeding,' she stated. The three women blinked for a moment before all three responded.

'You're old enough to deal with it yourself.'

'Put a Band-Aid on it.'

'If you got blood anywhere, you had better clean it up; it should look as though you were never there.'

'I'm bleeding because I got my period' Iesha spoke slowly, enunciating her words so that there would be no misunderstanding what she was talking about. The three women looked at her blankly; she thought she would need to repeat herself, and then they each spoke up, breaking the uncomfortable silence that had settled over them.

'It looks like you are finally a woman,' Carley said with a disinterested expression on her face.

'My father found me a husband when I became a woman,' her grandmother Maudereminisced with a slightly dreamy look in her eye and hum in her voice.

Interest entered Deirdre's eyes, and then she spoke, 'mmm, maybe there is some worth to you, yet.'

Resigned but not giving up, Iesha spoke again, her voice quiet but strong, 'I need supplies,' she hoped none of the women could see her nerves.

'Talk to your mother; girly' her grandmother waved her hand before picking up her cards and looking them over.

'You're a woman now; you can deal with it,' Carley crowed.

'Figure it out,' Iesha's mother, Deirdre, said with complete indifference. She, too, returned to her cards.

'Figure what out?" Tim's voice entered the conversation; he'd just gotten back after coaching basketball at the community and youth center.

'She is a woman' his estranged wife, Carley, cackled.

'What are you on about?' he raised an eyebrow and looked her like she was losing her mind.

'She has started her bleeds,' Maude stated before Carley could start ranting, 'she's all grown up now.'

'Okay, and what exactly does Iesha need to figure out?' his voice was calm, but he was not looking forward to their answers; no one spoke.

'How is everything, Iesha?" he knelt down until he was eye to eye with his niece.

Iesha took a deep, shuddering breath, 'i need supplies,' she repeated, this time speaking to her Uncle without looking at the women watching her.

Tim stood up, holding his hand out for her to take; she gripped it tightly. He then looked at the three women sharply and, in an icy voice, said, 'This I assume is what you've told Iesha to figure out by herself.'

The women looked at him, indifferent to the goings-on around them. He took a deep breath to calm himself, he felt Iesha squeeze his hand, and he breathed out.

'You know what they say about assuming, dear,'Carley drawled with sarcasm lacing her voice.

At the same time, Iesha's mother, his sister in law, responded, 'Yes.'

'You're all just going to sit there, aren't you?" he said, somewhat dumbfounded but mostly resigned to their actions.

'What else would we do?' all three women said; they had puzzled expressions and looked confused as to why he had asked the question at all.

"Right," he sighed; he squeezed Iesha's hand lightly before tugging it. He turned and headed for the door, her handheld comfortably in his, 'Come on, Iesha, let's go out and see if we can't buy you some supplies.'

It was the first time her Uncle bought her the supplies she needed, and it wasn't the last. From the point, he was the one to buy her supplies either when she ran out or needed to stock up.

He was her protector.

****

Carley, although unlikely her plan, gradually drove Iesha's Uncle Timothy out of the house. They became estranged but relatively normal. The investigation into the company that they had both worked for became more drawn out as the investigators uncovered more than embezzlement. In the end, it took three years altogether for both Carley and Timothy to be deemed innocent and non-complicit with the company's actions; both had been questioned a number of times over the period.

All of their accounts were released to them, and other than her personal account Carley shoved all the information and paperwork at Timothy and told him to deal with it; she was, after all, "too busy."

He asked if she was sure. Carley had scoffed and wandered away.

*

Timothy had gone over all the paperwork, made a couple of notes, and then hatched out a plan that would divide their joint accounts easily and remove his wife off his personal accounts. He was surprised that she had access to all his personal accounts while he had no access to her own account.

It infuriated him; they had agreed that their personal accounts were theirs and their joint accounts were shared and that they would both put money into it. He spoke with his lawyer and asked him to investigate all his account details and transactions – he wanted to know if they had both been depositing money throughout the history of their joint accounts and how much she had withdrawn from his personal accounts. He asked his lawyer what a divorce might involve and how he could go about it. He didn't file, but he did get his lawyer started on the paperwork – just in case.

*

He had the banking paperwork drawn up, his personal accounts returned to his sole control, and if Carley wanted money from their joint accounts, she would be allowed a set amount per month. He sat Carley down and explained all the paperwork – about her now limited access, and then he realized that she hadn't paid any attention to what he had been saying when she signed and didn't fight the decisions.

Deirdre had watched her sister; Timothy had looked at her while Carley was signing and raised an eyebrow; Deirdre had just smiled knowingly and known that Carley's life wasn't going to return to how it had been before the account was frozen. She had been boasting and gloating about how things would return to their rightful place.

*

Carley and Timothy continued to live in the house even though the accounts were once again active; Timothy had asked Deirdre if he could stay until he had everything organized. She had agreed, not minding or wanting him to leave because with him living in the house, she didn't have to spend any energy or thoughts on the child she had birthed and now wished was nothing more than a figment of her tired imagination.

***

Surprisingly it took her six months, but Carley was absolutely furious when she discovered not only the money limit but also that she no longer had access to her husband's accounts.

"What is this? Why have you done this to me, Timothy?" she whined, slamming the papers down in front of him at the table where he was sitting with Iesha working on her homework.

'Why did I do what, Carley?' he said tiredly.

'Look, why don't you look?' she whacked her hand against the papers repeatedly. Iesha shrunk slightly into her uncles' side and saw Deirdre's amused expression as she watched on.

Timothy collected the papers and looked over them, 'what is your problem with them, Carley? I sat down with you and explained everything that I had done and organized in regard to both my *personal* accounts and our joint accounts. You signed the paperwork, I filed it, and then we finally receive our reissued cards.'

'You did not explain this,' she screeched 'why is there a limit on what I can take out of our joint accounts? why don't I have access to the other accounts.'

'Yes, I did,' he stated

'Yes, he did,' Deirdre said at the same time, 'I witnessed the entire conversation and signed the papers as the witness.'

'Why didn't you say something?' Carley was really whining now.

"Timothy explained it twice, and you indicated that you had heard him both times. It is not either of our faults that you didn't listen to your husband's explanation. I'm also surprised you thought that things would return to normal," Deirdre was definitely amused now, for once Carley hadn't gotten her way.

'Fix it,' she demanded, glaring at Timothy.

'This is fixed' his voice clear and unwavering 'and turn off those crocodile tears. They lost their effect a long time ago.'

Carley's tears dried up, and she stomped her foot. 'Why?' she said childishly.

'In the months before all our accounts were frozen, you were withdrawing and spending more money from our joint accounts than you were contributing to them,' he began.

She interrupted him, 'But… I should get…'

He held up his hand, and Carley's voice spluttered to a stop; he continues, 'The other accounts you were drawing from were my personal accounts.'

'Timothy darling, you are my husband,' she said the words in a falsely sweet voice that mocked him as if that was all she had to do to get her way.

'And?' he looked at her as though she were stupid. She huffed.

'You are my husband; that means you provide for me, and I get access to the accounts. All of them.'

'Then I should get access to your account,' he responded blandly.

'That's personal. It's mine' she widened her eyes.

'Exactly, my *personal* accounts are mine. I don't have access to yours, and you don't have access to mine. When we opened the joint accounts, we had an agreement, which according to our bills and the records from before our accounts were frozen, you broke. So, I set a limit. You shouldn't have had trouble with the agreement we originally came to, you weren't earning that much less than me, and if we include those bonuses you received, sometimes you earnt more.'

'You can't,' she whined.

'I can. I have, and you signed the paperwork. It is not changing,' he spoke to her bluntly.

**

One month later, with no interactions or words other than Carley's overly dramatic sighing and excessive pouting. She handed him divorce papers, 'You made me do this. But you can still fix it,' she said, holding the papers out to him.

'I'll take these to my lawyer, and we'll look over them,' he said, taking the papers from her hand.

'Your lawyer,' she spluttered.

'Yes. You seem to have found yourself a lawyer; why wouldn't I have one of my own. Not only that, but you have clearly forgotten that one of my closest friends is a lawyer.' He looked at her with a placid expression on his face.

*****

Carley had eventually managed to find a job on the edge of the city center, but despite this and the access she now had to her personal accounts, she continued to live in the house with her sister Deirdre, Amos, and Maude.

She had been expecting a massive payout in the divorce, but Carley had received nothing, and she even had to pay her own lawyer bills. She was a woman who spent her money almost faster than she earned it. Cigarettes and alcohol – her money and her purchases only served to feed the problems within the house's walls.

****

When her Uncle Tim had started planning for after the divorce, he started by first looking for somewhere else to live. After Carley had filed for divorce, he had moved himself into the backyard. Iesha thought that his cozy cushion and blanket filled little green tent was like a great big nest.

During the divorce proceedings, Tim had sat down with the almost ten-year-old Iesha in his tent and explained that when the time came, he would be moving out completely and would no longer be camping out in the backyard. He explained that she would always be welcome in his home, and if he had anything to say or do about it, he would find a way for her to stay with him as much as possible, if not permanently – although this would take him longer.

'Really,' she asked, unable to keep the hope and excitement out of her voice.

"Of course. Now I need your expert eyes, I need to find a little house, and I need your help, especially if you'll be living with me too."

Iesha's face lit up, and she shifted excitedly on her cushion. Together they searched for somewhere for Timothy to live. Eventually, they narrowed it down, and on their weekends and on afternoons after school, she and Timothy viewed their choices. Finally, he made a decision and placed a bid. He received a positive response.

He breathed a sigh of relief; he had bought a house.

***

When her Uncle moved out of the house and into his own, the other adults of the house all said 'goodbye' in their own ways – all of them rude and offensive.

'Finally, wish you'd left years ago,' Amos said with a burp before taking a gulp of beer, not moving from his indent in the couch eyes still on the television.

'If I had, Iesha would have probably died in your care; hell maybe you'd be in jail for neglect and manslaughter,' Tim returned snidely.

'Yeah, right. We wouldn't go to jail.'

'I wish' Tim mutter in a low whisper that was only heard by his niece who was hugging him; she giggled into his stomach.

'Pity that your absence from this house leaves no extra room,' Maude said, knitting badly in an armchair; she was missing stitches. She had only started knitting because she had seen Tim teaching Iesha and had then ranted about how he couldn't be teaching her because he was a man and obviously didn't know anything. He had informed her that his grandmother had taught him before asking if she knew how to knit. She had flown into a huff and then marched off. The next time he had seen her, she had been sitting primly in a seat with gleaming knitting needles and bland colored yarn.

'Do get out, ex-husband, you aren't welcome here,' Carley drawled from her place beside Amos on the couch that she had once sneered at the sight of.

Dierdre scowled slightly, 'You might be leaving, but you're still taking the brat to school and picking her up. Don't forget.'

'I have no intention of forgetting.'

'Good! Everyone here is busy,' she said.

*****

A month later, Iesha had been spending a lot of time at her Uncle's home instead of the house she'd grown up in.

One night when they were eating dinner that she had been ordered to cook, both her biological parents said, 'God, get out, leave' and 'Why don't you just move out already?'

She told her Uncle the next morning on the way to school, and he had responded with, 'I'll figure something out so that you don't have to live in or serve the people living in that house.'

'Promise?' she asked.

'Pinkie promise,' he stated, holding his pinkie out to her.

Five days later, her Uncle knocked on the front door,

'What are you doing here?' his ex-wife screeched.

'I'm here about Iesha,' he stated.

'What's she done?'

'Why?'

'Why would you want to do that?'

He held up a stack of papers, 'all you have to do is sign these,' he said.

'What are they for?' Deirdre said suspiciously.

'I'm filing for full custody of Iesha. These papers are the easiest way for you, the unappreciative lot that you are, to get Iesha out of this house and your lives. If you don't sign these, I'm taking you to court.'

'We are not signing,' sneered Amos.

'You won't be granted custody.'

'Yes, I will,' he said without hesitation.

*

They didn't sign the papers, and her Uncle Tim did as promised. He took her biological parents to court, and then he proceeded to win full custody.

Chapter 3
Learning and Surviving – in scenes

Iesha liked school; she loved knowledge and learning; it was exciting if she came across something new to learn or to research.Before she had moved to live with her Uncle, school meant that she wasn't in the house that she had lived in for as long as she could remember – the house that she should have been able to call home.

Iesha had very vague memories where Amos and Deirdre, her parents, were reading to her, but they were few and far between. The memories had been overwritten by her memories of her Uncle reading to her. She didn't really remember the time before her Uncle was the one to put her to bed, to read to her, to make sure she went to sleep, and to deal with her nightmares as he saw fit.

Timothy read her fiction that fell in all the genres that he could think of; he read the classics, fantasy, science fiction, paranormal, adventure, and crime novels. He was the person who introduced her to the wonders of the library – a place where facts, breakthroughs, friendships, love, adventure, and magic thrived.

*

When Iesha was talked down to and insulted because of her gender, her Uncle introduced her and guided her to books about inspiring females. She learned about:

- the adventurer and pioneer of women's rights Amelia Earhart, the first woman to fly solo across the Atlantic.

- tennis player Billie Jean King, an advocate of equal rights, defeated chauvinist Bobby Riggs in the tennis match known as the Battle of The Sexes.

- Rosa Parks, who in 1955 sparked a turning point in the civil rights movement in America when she refused to give up her seat on a bus even though she was legally obliged to when asked by a white person.

- Helen Keller, the first blind and deaf person to earn a college degree – she was an author, lecturer, and political activist.

- Ada Lovelace (1815-1852) was considered by some to be the first computer programmer. She was a writer and mathematician who is most known for her work on friend Charles Babbage's proposed mechanical general-purpose computer called the Analytical Engine.

- and Marie Curie, the Polish physicist who conducted pioneering research on radioactivity and was the first woman to win a Nobel Prize.

**

When it was her race and the color of her skin that was held against her, her Uncle made sure that she discovered the lives of people who were famous and had made an impact and who happened to be of color. This meant that she was inspired by a range of men and women:

- Ruby Bridges, who at six years old, was the first African American to integrate the all-white William Frantz Elementary school located in Louisiana, she ate alone but never missed a day of school.

- Mary Fields (1832to 1914)was born as a slave and freed in 1865 – she was the first African American to work for the US postal service.Nicknamed Stagecoach Mary, she was hired as a mail carrier at the age of 63 when she was the fastest applicant to hitch a team of six horses. She was considered exceptionally reliable as she never missed work, and if her horses were held up by snow, she would put on snowshoes and deliver the mail by hand; she would carry the sack of mail over her shoulders.

- Phillis Wheatley(1753 to 1784)was born in West Africa and, as a young girl, was put on a ship and sent to the US, where she was sold as a slave to the Wheatley family. Her first name came from the ship she was transported in – Phillis. Unusual for the time, she was taught to both read and write. At the age of twenty, Phillis moved to England with her son – she published her first book within a year of arriving. She was the first African American to be published: for her first volume of poetry was published in 1773.

- Mary Seacole (1805-1881) was born in Jamaica and moved to England in the year 1854. She asked the War Office if she could go and help wounded soldiers who were fighting in the Crimean War (1853-1856), but she was refused. So, she raised the money herself and traveled to Balaclava, Ukraine, where she looked after the British soldiers who had been injured.

- Lilian Bader (1918-2015) was born in Liverpool and was one of the very first black women to join the British Armed Forces. She began working as a canteen assistant at the army base in Yorkshire. Eventually, she trained as an instrument repairer before becoming a leading aircraft woman, and then soon afterward, she went on to earn the rank of Corporal. She eventually left the army to have children, and she also completed a degree in teaching.

- Ignatius Sancho (1729-1780)was born on a slave ship.He was an orphan and a slave. He worked as a butler.The man who he worked for saw how clever he was and supported his creativity. He went on to eventually set up his own shop located in London, where creative people like him could meet up. Sancho wrote music, plays, and poetry. He is also known as the first black British voter.

- Ira Aldridge (1807-1867), he became well-known across Europe as a brilliant actor in Shakespeare's plays. Born in New York, he moved to England because he wouldn't have been able to achieve his acting goals in the United States. He was one of the highest-paid actors in the world at a time when black actors didn't have the same opportunities as white actors.

- John Edmonston (1792-1822) was born into slavery. When he gained freedom, he moved to Scotland, where he met Charles Waterton, a man who taught him the skill of taxidermy. Edmonston later became a teacher at Edinburgh University, where he went on to teach Charles Darwin.

- Martin Luther King Jr, minister, and activist. He became the most visible spokesperson and leader in the civil rights movement from 1955 until his assassination in 1968. He advocated civil rights through non-violence and civil disobedience. He is probably most well-remembered because of his 'I have a Dream…' speech that he gave in 1963 from the steps of the Lincoln Memorial.

- Booker T Washington (1856-1915)an author and orator who was an advisor for the American presidents Roosevelt and Taft. He advocated an incremental approach to improving education and the life prospects of black Americans.

**

When Timothy discovered that the teachers at her school were ineffectual, didn't seem to care for teaching, or to be more specific, they didn't care about the specific group of students that they had relegated to the class called 'special education,' he was furious.

He had waved his hands around, gesturing when he spoke to Iesha in a passionate voice late one evening.
'Those people, those teachers, are supposed to push their students to reach their potential, to climb great heights and embrace any abilities that they <u>do</u> have. Every child has potential and has something that they are good at. By treating you, and the others that they have deemed in need of 'special education, they are ignoring potential and only adding to the cycle of living that they themselves are judging you on. That school that Amos Deirdre and Maude sent you too, I have no doubt that your grandmother Maude was involved in the decision - they are judging you and your peers based on what neighborhood you come from, your gender, race, and skin color; they are doing nothing to improve your situations or encourage you to go further.'

****

One of the main rules, Iesha had decided, of surviving the house she had lived in, the school she first attended, and her original neighborhood was to: Watch, Learn, and DO. The attitude of what seemed to be the majority of people around her was negative and unhelpful, so she made the decision that if people wouldn't or didn't teach her that she could teach herself – she also learned that she could rely on her Uncle Timothy, she could ask him for help, and he would either teach her himself, or he would sit and learn with her.

*

She had started teaching herself to knit by watching the group of grandmothers at the community center - watching their weathered but nimble hands work the knitting needles – she hadn't asked if they would teach her, afraid they would be like her grandmother. Tim had found her tangled up with yarn scraps that she had collected and knitting needle she had obtained from the lost and found box at the center – he had offered to teach her, and she had been thrilled.

*

Iesha had started teaching herself to both read and write by watching her parents read to her; they used to let her fingers trace the words as they read them. When they stopped, she continued on her own until her Uncle arrived in her life and let her trail fingers across the words on the page and helped her sound out words and letters.

***

Iesha's backpack was covered in odd embroidery shapes, images, and patterns. She had been spending time at the community and youth center with her Uncle, both of them wanting out of that house, and one of the groups of crafters – bright-eyed little old ladies- had felt that the two of them needed to know how to sew, "It's a life skill, you know. Excellent for survival," Doris, the unofficial leader, told them as if it was one of the universe's big secrets. They had at first practiced on tea towels brought in by the ladies until one of the women had gifted Iesha with a backpack – it was made of grey fabric and had hardly been used.

Iesha had clutched it to her chest, her Uncle's hand on her shoulder,

'Thank you' they spoke at the same time.

'It's nothing dears, just something I had lying around and collecting dust,' the woman said with a grin, 'now the two of you can practice your stitches and your embroidery, and at the same time decorate the blank surfaces of your new bag.'

****

Most of what Iesha knew about cooking was learned from books beside her Uncle or from watching the cooks at her mother's work.

Between the ages of seven and ten, she had to spend time at Deirdre's work when there was no other option. At the diner, she was told to stay out of the way and to wash the dishes – it wasn't the best experience, but she did learn by watching the cooks, and she was paid under the table. Whether her parents, aunt, or grandmother allowed her to keep the money was an entirely different matter.

She supposed she sort of had her grandmother Maude to thank for knowing how to make fried chicken and chicken noodle soup – her grandmother had refused to teach her the recipes and methods she used but had told her that watching how she cooked both meals and staying quiet would teach her valuable lessons in patience.So, Iesha had stayed quiet and watched her whenever she made either meal.

*****

When Iesha had gone to her mother's work and had been put to work washing those dishes and wiping those tables, she was legally too young to be on payroll and had been paid money under the table by the owners of the diner. The moment she walked through the front door, her parents, grandmother, or her aunt would take them from her hands and pocket it.

Six months later, her Uncle arrived home early as all the adults were explaining why they were taking her money from her. She had tried to hide it and refused to hand it over, but they repeated the words that they had used the very first time they had taken her money.

'It means you are paying your way,' Amos and Maude said.

'That money will pay for your room and board, girl,' her aunt stated.

Her Uncle scoffed then held out his hand. 'If Iesha, who is a child, must pay for the room when she sleeps either on the floor the couch or the back porch, and board, why aren't you?'

'I'm family. Why aren't you?' she said

Deirdre snorted 'your husband pays for his own food, and he organized a price to pay as rent. He was paying for you in the beginning.'

**

After her Uncle had found out that her parents, aunt, and grandmother were taking the money she was given for working at the diner, Timothy took Iesha to the bank and organized a bank account under her name. The paperwork was filled out and signed, a deposit was made, and she had a bank account that was all her own. She had a place outside of the house where she could hide her money, collect it, and hoard it safely away from the greedy eyes and the sticky fingers belonging to her so-called family.

******

At her first school, she was learning nothing in her maths class. Her maths teacher seemed to prefer that her students just follow the instructions in the book without actually explaining anything, or she would write something on the board for them to follow before she sat and opened out a newspaper, a magazine, or a book and left the children to themselves.

In the end, her Uncle started teaching her about finance and numbers; he used real-world situations to help explain; when she understood numbers became easy, and when he finally convinced her parents to send her to a different school, he would sit with her when she worked through her maths work. If Iesha was sent to the store to do the shopping, she would add up the prices either in her head or on a scrap of paper.

**

Iesha watched other kids with their families, and by observing them, she learned about healthy or at the very least healthier family dynamics than her own. The other kids thought that she was quiet and weird, so instead of including her in their games, they left her behind and on her own. From her perch on a green bench at the side of the fields or from up on one of the tree branches in large oak, she witnessed and learned about teamwork, mediation, and even meditation – from the kids who would clench their fists and get angry before they would start muttering, close their eyes and begin taking deep breaths in and out.

***

It took her Uncle a couple of years to get Iesha's parents to agree for her to change schools, she was eight, and changing schools led to a change in the way that she was taught in the school setting. When her Uncle was teaching her, he realized that she was a visual and hands-on learner and that she found a book and wrote learning hard and that things didn't always make sense.

**

Iesha started dreaming of leaving the house of her childhood and the house that her parents lived in from about the age of eight. It began a fleeting notion and grew as she did. When her Uncle won custody, and she went to live with him, that dream became a reality. And it was like all those big dreams she had for the rest of her life might actually be a real possibility; having a place to belong and to call home, graduating high school, furthering her education, getting a job, being happy, succeeding, owning her own home and making an impact.

She was determined to be better, to be more than the assumptions and low expectations that people had laid on her. She wanted to be someone, bring about change – she wanted to be like her hero: her Uncle, and the father she chose, Timothy.

**

Iesha had always wanted somewhere that would be hers, that she wouldn't be kicked out of. She had thought that her bedroom had been hers until her aunt and

Uncle had appeared on their doorstep, and her aunt had demanded the space. Her Uncle had tried to find a different solution that involved something other than kicking her out of her own room.

She hadn't felt like she had had something of her own like that until her Uncle had moved into the house he bought and asked for her help in choosing it, the house where he had made one of the rooms for her, specifically. It was painted in her favorite colors and decorated in a way she adored. It had been the best (late) birthday present, for her tenth birthday, that she had received since her sixth birthday when her Uncle had given her her own set of classic novels that he then read to her.

*

When her Uncle Timothy had won custody, it had been like another present and had lifted her spirits. On her eleventh birthday, her Uncle offered her the chance at a new name and asked whether he could adopt her. She accepted both of his offers with her wild heart, feeling as though it was beating out of her chest. She was being given a chance to be whoever she wanted – she could name herself; her name could be anything. After much thinking, she had kept her first name and changed her middle name of Maudlin, which had been a tribute to her grandmother, to Motha and her last name was a change to match her uncles – Davies.

*

When the papers came through, stating her new name and the adoption approval, her Uncle had shown her the official papers while they were sitting at the little dining table. Iesha had stood from her chair and walked around the table to hug the man who had been pretty much raising her since he had arrived at her childhood home; he had given her a safe place to go when he moved out, who had then fought and gained custody of her. He might not be her father biologically, but he was her dad. She pulled back. "Can I call you, dad?" she blurted out.

His eyes widened in surprise

She tried to retract the statement

"Iesha, calm down; I would be honored to be called dad, just as I was honored that you called me Uncle. I have considered you my daughter for a number of years now."

"You've been my dad for a long time, I've considered you my dad in my head, but I was too scared of how <u>they</u> would have reacted if I'd said it in that house or worried that you'd refuse"

Timothy pulled her back into a hug and kissed the top of her head paternally. "You are my daughter. I am proud of you, never forget."

***

During the summer after she moved in with her Uncle, a group of her Uncle's friends decided that they wanted to set up their dual business - dealing with finances, accounting, and building and construction management– nearby.

Her Uncle volunteered to help them set up their premises – they were sharing the space, located about fifteen minutes from Timothy's house. Half of the space would be devoted to financing and accounting; the rest of the space focused on building and construction management.

***

Holding her uncles'hand, she nervously entered the building, her backpack on her shoulders filled with the thing they had thought he might need for the day. Her ever-present notebook and pens for her to write down her notes, thoughts, observations, and the odd sketch – being one of them.

Her Uncle's friends were waiting for them with smiles, coffee, and pastries. They were sitting on a picnic blanket on the floor of the space.

'Have to feed our helpers, don't we?' one of the men said with a wink.

'Iesha, that is Greg,' he pointed to the winking man, 'the man sitting next to him with the coffee clutched in both hands and looking dreamy is Harry – he is somewhat addicted to coffee.'

'Hey,' the man protested half-heartedly, 'I'm trying to make a good impression on your niece.'

'And such a marvelous job you're doing, looking at that coffee as if it had all the answers,' he drawled with amusement, and Iesha giggled at the expression on the newly introduced Harry's face. He puffed up and beamed at the sound.

'See, she likes me,' he said, looking proud.

'Or she thinks you're a silly bugger,' said a red-haired man with a slight accent.

Her Uncle snorted before continuing with his introductions 'The redhead with the accent is Irish, and his name is Damien, the lady of the group who also has red hair is Julia, and she is Damien's twin sister.'

'Hi, there,' Julia said softly; she held out her hand for Iesha to shake.

Iesha blushed at the attention but gave a small smile, waved one of her hands, and shook Julia's with her other.

Iesha and her Uncle ate pastries, drank hot chocolate and coffee respectively, and relaxed into the friendly atmosphere and cheerful chatter that they were being drawn into. The whole thing had Iesha blinking; it was different from the house or school – she had never been included in anything like this, and her Uncle was looking happier around adults than she had ever seen.

***

Iesha was asked to help organize files and any loose papers; they put her in one of the corners where there were good light and plenty of space, they put the boxes filled with paperwork around her. She found it soothing working with the paper and listening to her Uncle and the others moving things, chattering, and laughing.

She'd been sorting things for maybe an hour, and there was heavy lifting being done around her when she found a loose sheaf of papers with numbers that didn't make sense. This she found odd as since her Uncle had started teaching her maths, she had never had a problem, and they had always made sense.

An hour and a half later, they-Timothy, Greg, Harry, Damien, and Julia – found Iesha sitting cross-legged and deeply focused.

She had a blue pen behind done ear, a black pen shoved into her hair and a red pen behind her other ear; there was a pencil in her hand, and she was scribbling away in her notebook. They looked at her silently; Damien nudged Tim,

'What's she doing?' he asked curiously.

'Damien, you should be asking if she's okay,' Julia hissed at her brother.

Tim snorted. 'She's fine, focused on the numbers. I'd say she found a problem amongst your papers that she felt needed solving.'

'What sort of problem? I thought all our papers were good.'

'After she understood all the basics and the not so basics of mathematics, she hasn't had a problem with numbers. Sometimes she sees things that others might not,' Timothy said, almost on the defensive.

'Relax, you told us she was a little genius, and you aren't one to exaggerate. I'm just wondering what she found.'

'Oh, sorry. A lot of people are dismissive of her, and it pisses me off' He rubbed a hand through his hair before stepping forward and slowly sitting down opposite Iesha. He hummed and tapped his fingers on her notebook. She looked up and sort of held her breath and started blinking rapidly.

'Breathe,' he said in a calm voice. She gasped out a breath, and then gradually, her breathing evened out.

'Hey there, kiddo, looks like you got a little lost in the numbers.'

'Problem,' she stated succinctly.

'I thought so; how about you have some water? I'd say you got carried off in your problem solving and haven't had anything to drink since you started,' he began, 'Is it okay if the others sit with us?'

'The floor is free,' she said, nodding and drinking from her water bottle.

There were laughs as the others sat down.

'Iesha, when you're ready, can you explain what you found for us?'Timothy asked.

She nodded and opened her mouth.

***

When the businesses opened, they asked her if she would eventually like a job working with them. She had nodded; she began when she and her Uncle visited – she would do odd little jobs or look at the number. When the job became official, she fourteen, and she did a number of things in the offices: transferring phone calls, taking messages, filing, any odd jobs, and they still asked her to double-check numbers when they were dealing with a lot of them.

As her Uncle had told them, Iesha might have been young, but numbers made sense.

****

To most people, Iesha was invisible, either that or they looked at her and judged – they saw what she was and not who she was. All they saw was that she was African American, that she was female, that she was poor and from a bad neighborhood.

One of the teachers at the first school she attended had said to her Uncle in a superior tone of voice, 'Oh, please, the girl's a nobody, and she won't ever be somebody,' she paused, 'Don't look at me like that at least I can say that I haven't been filling her head with the impossible.'

'You haven't been filling her head or any of your student's heads with anything.'

'They're 'special education' that means that they're not worth it.'

'That is bullshit,' he said bluntly.

'We are talking about your niece, not the other kids, and the only way she will ever be somebody is if that girl somehow miraculously becomes a success. Which obviously won't happen.'

*

But Iesha was persistent, determined, and driven, and she wanted to make her uncle/dad proud. I wanted to be more than her situation. She wanted to be more than the world and life that she had been born into. She knew that a part of her would always want to prove her naysayers wrong, and while money would be nice, she saw money as less important; it meant more to her to have a positive impact, to achieve something, and feel safe.

**** ****

Living with her Uncle Tim, being in his custody, made her life easier, and she found school easier to deal with. She no longer had to return to spend any time in the house of her childhood – the house where she was treated like a servant, an inconvenience, a thing.

****

Iesha decided that she wanted to be a real estate agent in her last two years of high school. The idea had started brewing in her mind as she worked in the offices for the dual businesses- finance/accounting and the building and construction management business – that her dad's friends ran. She was learning and had learned a lot in those offices, and it had sparked many ideas of what she could do in her future. It was interestingly, advertising that solidified the notion of becoming a real estate agent. Various real estate agencies and individual agents were promoted on posters, across billboards, and on signs attached to public seating.

There was one advertisement in particular that stuck in her mind. It was simple but bold; a woman stood in a sleek suit; her smile was bright and friendly against her caramel-colored skin. Iesha had sucked in a sharp breath when she had seen them because there was an ad with a female who had colored skin looking happy and successful. Iesha wanted to be that woman: with a confident posture, smile, and air of success.

***

Iesha knew that there were people living in her neighborhood and in the surrounding neighborhoods whose rent was raised in an effort to 'clean up' the suburbs. The idea was to raise the cost of housing and rent in the area, thus creating what would be perceived as a good neighborhood and improving the reputation and 'cleaning up.' To turn this idea into reality, they were charging more and raising prices, which was making things less affordable. They were treating the current occupants and people of the area badly and unfairly - as if their lives were of little value- they were offering next to no money to the current owners of the properties they were buying up. In fact, they offered well under the market value, and they said that these people would be guaranteed a new home in the brand new buildings and housing that they would be building. The expense and extra cost that they would need to pay in order to guarantee a place for them to live in were never mentioned.

*

As she was growing up, Iesha had seen this scheme happen more than once. She had seen not just individuals but families with children end up on the streets because of greed, indifference, and uncaring attitudes.

**

Uncle Tim inspired her to be generous and to help people. As more people ended up homeless due to high housing costs, they organized the community and youth center to be used as a soup kitchen and then as a homeless shelter at night. They put work into the community and youth center trying to create and arrange a safe place; it took time and a lot of hard work, but the ideas came to fruition, and they were a success.

The soup kitchen and shelter angered some people, the same outsiders who were responsible for the increased presence of homeless people living outside on the streets and in the cold.

She remembered asking why the outsiders hadn't and didn't make affordable and safe housing. Her Uncle and his friends sat with her and explained how there were some people out there in the world who didn't care about safe buildings, so they cut corners; there were people for whom money and profit was the aim; it was about making money or saving money where they could.

*

When the idea first began building in her head, Iesha had visited the library. She had looked for books on real estate, becoming a real estate agent, and the connections to property development. She sat down with the pile of books she had collected and started to go through them one by one, taking detailed but succinct notes as she worked. After she'd gone through the books, she turned to computers and the internet. At this point, her research really took off and diversified.

*

She and her Uncle had sat down for dinner and were talking about this and that when he asked, 'What would you like to do after you leave school when you grow up?'

Iesha took a deep breath and bundled her courage before speaking.

"I was thinking of being a real estate agent," she spoke in a sort of rush, the words tumbling from her mouth. She could feel her nerves skyrocket, and panic began to set in.

"Just breathe, Iesha. Everything is okay," her Uncle spoke up, his voice immediately soothing and calming her nerves.

"I was thinking," she repeated, then she paused. "No,' she took a deep breath, 'I want to be a real estate agent."

"Do you have a plan for achieving that goal?" he asked, not questioning her choice of job.

"Do you think I can?" Iesha twisted her hands together in front of her.

"I have no doubt that you can achieve whatever you put your mind to. Is there anything I can do to help?"

"Thank you," She breathed out.

****

Iesha worked hard to achieve her goal of becoming a real estate agent. She researched what further education she would need, the state requirements, what the various fees were, were there exams she needs to take? And what sort of licensing would she need to become an agent. Her job at the offices paid well, and she had been saving since her Uncle had organized a bank account for her. She had no trouble paying to take a pre-licensing course. She found and chose the pre-licensing course that was best for her in terms of learning style and fitting into her work and study schedule. She had to seriously consider each course because the quality of the instructors and the materials would influence her success and her preparation for taking the licensing exam.

Over the course of her studies, Iesha studied the various areas and things that a real estate agent has to deal with day to day, like showing homes to prospective buyers, helping with property valuation, mortgages, financing, and government programs.

When Iesha had finished the course, it was time to take the exam. She registered and paid for the scheduled exam, which was computerized and would be in two parts, and Iesha knew that she had to pass both parts of the exam to become licensed.

****

When she got her license, her dad made a reservation at a nice restaurant and took her out for dinner. During the meal, she talks excitedly about sending out her resumé and finding a job. He tells her it might take time but to remain strong.

**

Iesha sent out her resumé to all the real estate agencies to those that are looking for new hires, looking for people who are wanting to start in the business. Not all her resumés are sent; she also visits agencies in person - looking to gain a job and experience in her field.

She received a variety of replies and responses; unfortunately, negative and rude seemed to be a common theme.

*

On one occasion, she had been called in for a job interview; the minute the interviewers had seen her, their eyes had widened, but they had ushered her into the office and close the door before speaking to her.

"We don't hire people like you?" they said bluntly.

"Like me?" she raised an eyebrow.

"Yes. Thank you for understanding" they all smiled and nodded, indicating to the door. She stayed sitting, and each of the interviewers looked confused and irritated.

"I don't understand. Why exactly can't you hire me?" she asked point blankly and then waited for their answer.

"We don't hire real estate agents who are inexperienced," the eldest interviewer said, her grey hair pulled back tightly; her male companions nodded in agreement.

"Your job advert asked for newly licensed applicants. It welcomed those people for 'learn on the job' experience. You advertised joining an enthusiastic team."

"Ahh," the men said simultaneously.

'I'd forgotten about that,' muttered the woman, none too quietly.

'Probably shouldn't have said that. If you were trying to say that discretely, you failed,' Iesha noted the amusement on the face of one of the men; she stood up and then glared icily at the interviewers, 'I would have preferred honesty rather than your excuses and lies.'

Iesha strode out of the office with her head held high.

**

Eventually, she found a job that sounded promising at a real estate agency on the edges of the city and just under an hour away from her home, where she still lived with her dad. She applied for a job, a little let down by the others she had applied for but crossing her fingers and hoping for the best. She was called in for an interview, and a day later, she was offered the job. Even though she had the job at the estate agency, she still helped out at the offices that she had been officially working at since she was fourteen. Her Uncle, now dead, and his friend was her family and her support – she loved spending time with them, and if they asked her to look over some numbers, she found the familiar actions relaxing her.

*****

It took her two years to realize that if she wanted to change things in the outer suburbs and neighborhoods that she'd grown up in and around, that she would need to start her own business to do so.

*

She continued working at the agency that had given her first job in the business. She worked hard, was exceptionally good at her job, was respected by her clients, and she was paid well. In her spare time, Iesha started building her business; and it began with her aims and wishes for her company.

Her real estate business would need to have community-oriented people with a drive to create change, who were loyal and enthusiastic. She would also need to invest in properties and buildings to create income and to help pay for improvements and create an affordable living. She felt that a real estate agency with investment properties was a smart and sound part of her plan.

*****

After three years and the agency, Iesha bought herself a little house in a nice neighborhood that was halfway between her work at the edge of the city and her dad's house. The house wasn't anything more than a fixer-upper. The building was watertight, but there were many tasks that needed to be done. The walls needed fixing; it looked as though someone had played whack a mole and filled it with holes; the electricity and plumbing needed to be checked and possibly upgraded – she made a note on her list that Julia and Damien might be able to help her find the right people to do that job; and there was also a lot of cleaning and other fixing that was needed. But using the connections that she had, she soon had turned her purchase into a cozy home.

She had bought and now owned her own 'estate'; it was small, but like a character from Jane Austin'snovel Pride and Prejudice, the ownership of the property had was a statement and had meaning; it definitely did for her.

Owning her own home had been a dream since Iesha was nine and strengthened just before when her Uncle had divorced her aunt and moved out.

****

When she had decided that she wanted to start her own business, she had thrown the idea out at the dinner table, surrounded by her dad and his friends who had become her uncles and aunt. Her uncles had handed her dad twenty dollars each.

"What?" she the words stuttered out in astonishment.

"Your dad here, bet that you'd want to open your own business within the first three years of you working at that real estate agency that gave you a job."

"The three of you made a bet I'd want to go out on my own in the world of real estate within three years," she questioned, raising a neatly curved eyebrow.

"Your dad bet within three years, but we made the bet that it would be within five years, not three," Julia said dryly.

"Will you help me?" Iesha asked; these were the people who had helped teach her that asking for help was not only allowed but also encouraged. It was a happy reminder that she wasn't alone and that she could ask for help.

****

After she had the realization that she needed to start her own business in order for her to achieve her goals of affordable living, it took her almost three years of careful planning and research to set everything up and for her to start her own real estate business.

It was unbeknownst to her the beginning of an Empire.

***

So, the process started. Iesha first went about things by creating a detailed but straightforward business plan. Once that was complete, she was able to map out her business's exact goals, their niche, and come up with a name for her company.

Next came registering the business, and once that came through, she quit her job at the real estate agency she had been working at and found an office space to work from; her dad - Tim, Damien, and Julia had accompanied her on her property search, she trusted them and their opinions would be helpful.

Once she had a premise, Iesha put out an advert and started putting a small team together, making sure to consider every applicant carefully. Her family invested some of their money to help her get started, and it also helped that some of her previous clients had left the other real estate agents to use hers.

In the beginning, she hired two people, who shared her beliefs in affordable and safe living, and the team of three sets to work. Once they had new clients coming in, Iesha sat down and looked at finances – not only the companies finances but her personal finances.

Then with the help of her employees, she sat down and looked at properties for sale- trying to decide what to invest in first.

They need to be the right properties; these first properties were going to be rented out, and the income they created would go into buying a property that could be turned into affordable housing.

The whole purpose and their main aim were to create affordable living in neighborhoods where greed had in the past left people on the streets. The new homes needed to be airtight, safe, and comfortable – because there were those who had been denied those comforts.

She wanted to help the communities that didn't have what the people in the city had. Iesha loathed domestic violence, abuse, and homelessness; she loathed seeing the hunger in people's eyes, especially in the eyes of children. This drove her further in her efforts to improve things for people her were suffering. She worked at rehoming the homeless and organized programs to get people back on their feet. She would give jobs or find jobs for those who needed them. She opened doorways and provided chances to people who may not have been given them at any time before.

**

And perhaps, one day, she would become an inspiration for young girls like she had once been.

****

<u>The woman who became a mogul to help the community she came from</u>

Iesha Motha Davies was born Iesha Maudlin Jackson, a little African American girl whose childhood was marred by slurs, neglect, and violence. But there came a lantern in her dark world in the form of her mother's sister's husband – her Uncle, Timothy Davies. Timothy began as her Uncle, but he quickly became her carer, teacher, confidant, and eventually, her dad. He gave her strength, happiness, and a family.

Now she has the chance to change lives as her dad changed hers; she is taking the opportunity to be a light and help improve the lives of others.

<u>PROFILING</u>

Iesha Motha Davies

This inspirational woman began work washing dishes as a child; then, she was given a job at a dual business that was in part finance/accounting and in part building and construction management. She studied hard and became a real estate agent. She faced discrimination on all fronts, and it took time for her to find a job–although eventually, she did. She spent five years working with them before leaving their employment.

With her business now registered, all she needed to do was get it up and running.

She started as just a real estate agent, and now she's both an agent and business owner. As business progressed and she became a licensed real estate investor and a broker.

She is now a real estate mogul and a passionate entrepreneur who spends her time creating affordable, comfortable, and safe housing in areas that were once considered bad and not worth the time. But Iesha is of humble beginnings; her birth was natural and ordinary – happening in a poor neighborhood. She was bullied and belittled but found a family that supported her, and she grew strong in mind and character. She is a helpful and caring member of the community. Now she sits on a self-made throne, as Queen of business. A Natural Born Queen.

www.ingramcontent.com/pod-product-compliance
Lightning Source LLC
Chambersburg PA
CBHW051938150726
47999CB00006B/2273